Poemlets
16

Cherry Books

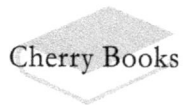

The 2016 Collection

Foreword

I am always envious of those who can combine critical and creative writing – for me, my day job of analysing literature seems to have contributed to the withering away of my admittedly nascent and juvenile creative writing. There is no reason why it should be so – it is not like critical writing does not require a certain kind of creativity, and as the pages of this book show, it is perfectly possible for people to be equally proficient, and equally passionate about these two apparently very different worlds.

The pages of Poemlets 16 show very different worlds in another sense as well. These poems vividly demonstrate how global a language English has become. To say this in 2016 is not to say something radical or new – postcolonial literature and world literature are now established disciplines of study in almost all English departments around the world. This is, of course, as it should be. But the last few months have also seen metaphorical shutters closing down, and real borders tightening as country after country in Europe, Australia and America enact ever more draconian immigration laws in a misguided attempt to recover some long-lost mono-cultural past. These policies are, of course, more than misguided – they are dangerous and are making the lives of all those who live in othered margins even more precarious.

This is the context in which I read these poems – this book as a whole, for me, powerfully articulates the right to claim the English language, and therefore the whole world that has helped to create it, as one's birth right. It reminds me how futile it is to police the borders of nations and cultures. It gives me hope that those who seek to shut down the windows of their societies to foreign people, influences and ideas are on the wrong side of history.

As 2016 comes to an end, I cannot think of a more important, or a more necessary reminder than this.

Dr Anindya Raychaudhuri
School of English
University of St Andrews

Editor's Note

Poemlets 16 is an endeavour to showcase the poems of academicians from around the globe; profuse expressions of thoughts and feelings, which seek to bond with emotions beyond the ordinary powers of comprehension.

I do not wish to glorify or impose my own impressions about the authors and their poems but am truly convinced that as you journey through this book it will grab you by the heart, linger there forever and never let you go.

Sheeba Thattil
Editor

Contents

Aswathy Balachandran

I Wish To Be Naked

Oh God! Undo this
I am cloaked in scorching memories
Let me be naked.
I see a little girl in red frock
Sitting on her mother's lap
Unaware of the selfish world outside
She grows into a pretty girl in her teens
Babbling to her peers under the shade
And later sharing her dreams to that someone
She will lose for ever
I see her amidst the chaos of life
She is a wife, and a mother too
Her chastity replaces her identity
Her son suckles, her white blood oozes
I see her in her husband's cemetery
Chanting, the beads held tight in her hands
Ready to journey to the "rest-house"
As her only son calls it
Oh God! Am I this woman?
Please remove the cloak
I wish to be naked.

Flash

The photographs in the album look pale
Time has fashioned distorted shapes
And blurred images on the black pages
 Our broken relationships...
This photograph taken in a hill station looks ashen
Cousins, uncles and aunts
Stand around my grandparents
Partially covered by a drifting mist
A mist that later blocked our minds.
My favourite photograph is frayed at the edges
My sister hugging me tightly
As if she never wanted to lose me,
But somewhere along the way
Haven't we lost each other?
I wake from my memories
To the harsh truth that dawns
My own children may seek me
In the vanishing glory of an antique album.

Memories

The light has gone out
Only the murky pyre
Near his favourite mango tree;
He had touched her fingers
With a loaded eye
Like he did many years back
When they exchanged the rings
Before another flame.
She sat silently in "their" room
Weighed down by the pangs
Of the irrevocable, but inevitable,
The children kissed their mother
Only to go back to their roles
Of husbands, wives and parents.
She remembered that day
When they had sprouted as strangers
Later blossomed and entwined into one soul;
She recollected their pretty petty quarrels
Her preference of red to his blue
The hidden turbulence inside
When they were away from each other
The sparkle in his eyes when he was told
Of the stirrings of his blood in her womb;
And a glitter for the second time
As they hugged their first grandchild together.
She lay down on his blue shirt
Clinging to the scent
She has lost for ever
A whole long life and moments together
Only the memories of a life lived together.

Songs Of Peace

The bygone past never comes back
To remind us of its sweet fragrance
The baffling present sears the mind
Men unleash the beast in him
Wars turn the garden of love
Into large pools of blood
The cries of bereaved mothers
Wane into hopeless sobs
And the ebullient childhood
Loses its vigour and meaning
But can't we hope for a good morrow?
Let's sow the seeds of forgiveness and love
And pluck the blossom of a bright future
Where radiant men sing
Songs of everlasting peace.

Beena Job

Under My Wings Of Mercy

Sometimes it's hard to understand,
Sometimes I wonder why
Even in the midst of a crowd I am so alone,
And those nearest to me seem so far away.
Sometimes I'm lost inside of me,
Sometimes I just can't see;
I'm so weary and worn, I can find no rest,
My joyless heart is put to test.
When my life begins to fall apart,
Then I hear Your whisper in my heart.

Come let me hold you in a warm embrace,
Chase the shadows I see upon your face;
For under the wings of my mercy,
You're sheltered and safe from all worry;
And under the wings of my mercy,
You shall abide and sing for joy.

Geethanjali Kurian

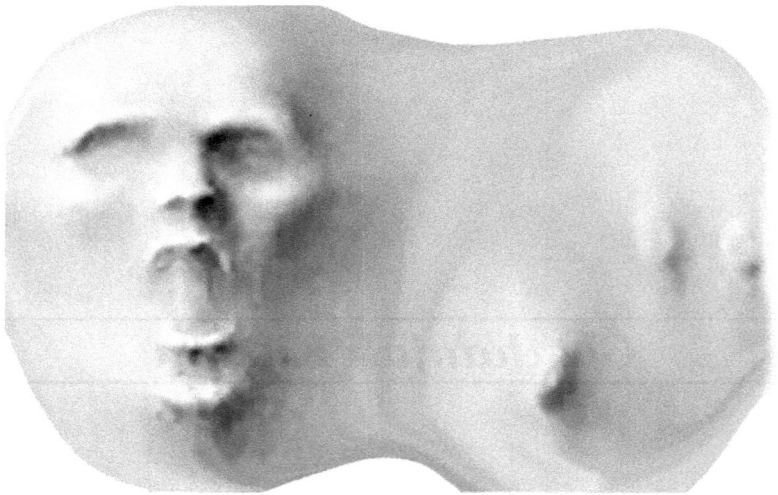

I Used To See Dead People

I used to see dead people

Each night spent in the musty embrace
of an antique four poster, draped with the dust of a century
Icy wraiths scented with aged lavender
like grandmum's talcum

Strangers at first
reaching out to touch
my skin snap frozen
my mouth wide in screams only I could hear

In the morning I would strain to remember
if the wraiths had faces

Was one a woman
her pale curls falling from a parting that bled
blue eyes set in mother of pearl
white muslin gown caught in a breeze I could not feel

Was there a little boy, pleated shorts held up
by suspenders that fell down his chubby arms
spoilt mouth pouting in discontent
eyes watery with need for something he could not have

Did I see the man from the daguerreotype that hangs in the
drawing room
extending to me his pocket watch
its hands arrested at 11:45
his pleading eyes sitting oddly in a fierce face

Each night they came until
strangers became friends
mutual comfort forged in silence
Who are you I asked them one day
Did you once live here father, mother and son

Were u the lady of this manor, draped over the chaise lounge
embroidering tea roses on a tapestry
stretched taut over a wooden frame
while turbanned footmen with rebellious eyes served you tea

Were you her child, chattering in the nursery
to your plain jane governess
spending her abandonment teaching you to read
secretly telling you tales of pimpernels
and pirates and thieves

Were u the lord of this manor
Striding in at eventide triumphantly
fondling the calling card of a continental prince
you met at the gentlemen's club

Did she float in then, night gown translucent
to lay on this bed, canopy drawn
as you pulled the drawstring and
trailed the french brandy down her breast

Were u happy here in this vaulted mausoleum
now weeping untold history

Was the stark whitewash of these walls
then papered china blue chinoiserie
replete with birds of paradise
jostling portraits of stern ancestors
with yapping hounds at their heels

Was the dusty library polished mahogany
the scent of fine cigars and finer gentlemen
clinging to a marching band
of gold tooled, leather clad tomes

Did drapes of thin lace. swagged in green velvet
frame windows that spied
on extravagant white peacocks
who put paid to delusions of delicacy
with harsh braying cries, that animated regimented flower beds

But they said nothing my wraiths
not a word nor nod nor blink they deigned
my imaginings unworthy, my questions unsound
Illusory sentinels only I could see
Until the night they came no more

I used to see dead people

This Will Now Be My Place

This will now be my place
This will now be my space
My roots must drive deep
my branches flourish sheltering
my own

But I am no native
my intentions are suspect
For
here
belongs to one who is of this land
I am furtive
wondering if he will
hold me to account, ask me to leave

But the one who is of this land sees me not
He remains unseen
roaming the fringes of the outlier
fenced out by new rulers
who rode in on waves
his land then assailed
its red earth smudged to pale

I see him not amongst the million
with whom I jostle to seek my place
pandora pulsing from lands beyond proverbial seas
gravity slips them down to the tip
to this land
unknowing
that they too must seek
validation from him who is of this land

But how can they
when he remains without
silenced dictated told held scolded
by sea pirates
He is
errant never sighted

And I like the million am comfortably
blind deaf mute
furtive
jostling to cleave my roots deep
cunning parasite with no permit

Guilt is a haze
ignored until
I see him one day
there in the outlier
dark burnished brown
dusted with red
proud silhouette
unbent
wordless

Even if he speaks
even if I speak
it would be but noise
for I know not the language
of his people
which echoes with the urgent song
of hot winds
Guttural primordial cadence
of ancient red earth

Instead I spent a lifetime
learning the flat rude dissonance of
the pale riders new tongue
so I could seek out the usurpers
who I knew could now deign
to grant me leave
to seek my place to seek my space
here
which really is not my place

But I never planned to seek his leave
he who is of this land
who sees me from the outlier
patiently waiting to be asked
I am ashamed

Kaleidoscope

In the fullness of time
will I finally see the parade of happenstance
in a kaleidoscope gone mad

Odd shards of glass shaping moments
some clear, pure, transparent blue
others coloured green, shimmering hopeful beads
and thin opaque yellow lightless bangles
next to dripping threads of red and amber glass

Each shake an abstraction
Shifting, random reflections
Odd shapes trip together
imprisoned
restless in a chamber of mirrors

Never still, never the same
a tumbling endless parade of gaudy happenstance

Bend In The River

There is a
bend in the river
a curve wrought by the woods
that crowd her flanks, skew her lines
eager to touch cool waters
Trees lean languidly
their lethargy stirred by the susurrus of a quiet breeze
a clamour of crows converse uncaring of the sylvan scene
Sheep graze the incline over on the other side
their shepherd lies dreaming a ripple away from the water's edge
his turban tilted over his eyes
The faint sound of bells heralds his beloved
her anklets betraying her pretence of stealth
There in the shadow of the leaning bower
hidden from all but the river
the lovers hold hands, flirting in whispers
until the breeze shifts
and the river turns dusky reflecting the trail of the fleeing sun
The lovers leave leading a procession of bleating sheep
crows fly to distant roosts
The river now heavy, her waters heave
the lightness of day seduced in the stillness of night

Joe Poonolly

Half Past

The fire inside has subsided
Silhouettes of the ember barely glow
The core has thinned to its fiber
My shriveled body is withering away.

Like the last leaf, life flutters
Ebbing to leave this frail frame.

Yet memories do thrive
Dreams keep churning
In some obscure deep crevasse
Of a mind that refuses to age.

Like the new lit flame, mind flitters
Jumping out of this frail frame.

Will another bud ever sprout
Will I get my paddle back
Is there a shore near to reach
Or is it time to dissolve into oblivion?

O.J Joycee

Working Mother

Soft, oozing rubber
Deceived the li'l one
Stifled his cry
Beguiled his thirst
Silenced his whine.
A few bus stops away
His nourishment
Cuddled a computer
That crooned lullabies
From nine to five.
At six
Swollen breasts released
Stale manna—
Relief at last—breast or babe?
As each fought the duel
God wondered
Have I erred?

Lakshmi Russell

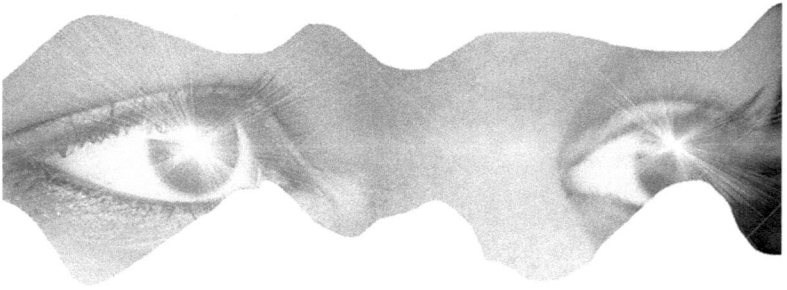

The End Of The World

In the darkness I searched for light
The light that was about to be eclipsed
There were cries of hatred, loss and pain
Desperate cries of hopeless agony.

Blind with lust, anger and greed
We cannot see on whom we tread
A spur of the moment or endless blindness?
One little knows why this act of unkindness

The umbilical cord that holds us together
By man and nature is seldom remembered
Would the world end in clashes and war?
Or simply leave it to natural calamities?

In the darkness I searched for light
And found that I am the light
In the darkness I searched for light
And found that light in each of my readers.

The Multifaceted Life

Life is like sports
Like cricket, badminton and boxing
Of unleashing and defending

Like math
Every problem has a solution

Like physics
Every action has an equal and opposite reaction

Like chemistry
Of composing matters that are a mystery

Like commerce
Of profits, losses and training in business

Like banking
Of fixed deposits and accounting

Like literature
The retelling of untold stories

Like psychology
Mind and intellect discern the personality

Like history
Thoughts, feelings and actions
Lead to one's destiny

Life is a drama
Of peripetia and anagnorisis
Leading to climaxes

When life ends
God asks one nothing, save
Was your life worth living?

Latha Nair R

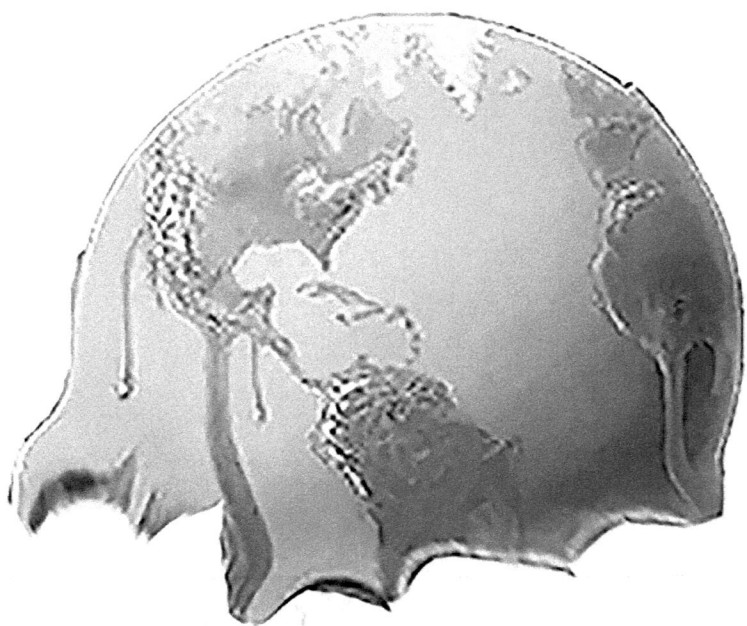

Earth's Silent Song

Have you ever listened
To the silent voices in nature
That speaks about the promise of life
And the earth's plea to be heard?

Have you ever listened to the murmur in the winds
Or the wings budding on an insect's back,
Looked for the footprints of a wee little bird
Or the world's reflection in the eye of an ant?

Only after death do we tend to listen
To earth and its sorrowful insinuations,
Grasp a copy of the hueless picture
And the dull shadow of a fading rainbow.

Then man, the lord of long slumber
Learns to listen, not just with his ears
But his whole body, pressed to the earth,
The sad, silent music of the dying earth.

Lisa John

Stench

The stench
Of new life
Of fresh air
Of pure water
Of pristine pastures.

The stench
Of profound love
Of genuine succour
Of unflinching words
Of cordial haptics
Of unshrinking fidelity
Of inviolable trust
Of unfeigned honesty.

The stench
Of laughter
Of coyness
Of contentment
Of ecstasy.

Earth reeks
Of life.

Lovji KN

Between The Sky And The Sea

Higher and higher in a spiral
Flapping my wings to gain altitude
I soar above the storm clouds,
And dare the freezing wind
To arrive at the star studded skies.
I swoop down into the water
In search of a safe landing
Amidst the brawling sea,
And circle the helpless tide
To arrive at the water's brim.
They call it an illusion
The meeting of the sea and the sky,
But we have shared ages and ages
The sky, the sea and I.

Mabel Susan

Love's Fall

Harden me against the biting cold
Thicken the streams of sap
Firmly let my roots grip the ground
Hold me steady in the storm
Strip me of these golden leaves
For this is me Love's Fall.

Close

Frozen
Channel
Red rivers stream down
Flecks, sanguine on the snow
Christmas

Stiff
Wooden
Snow white gown
Cross between folded fingers
Lifeless

Dead
The songs
Chants on the lips of a mother
Frankincense, the odour at bay
Candles

Sombre
Prayers
Peer down, the gravel hits the wood
Stifled sobs here and there
Closed.

Mallika A Nair

Lament Of A Lone Loser

Let there be seeds from bundles of sheaves
Let there be music by earthy crickets,
Sweet and scented harvest songs
To frame the fragrance of love profound.

Lend me a bow to shoot an arrow
And carry my thoughts to another tomorrow,
Let earth that's dearer than dear life to me
Be granted as hope to infants of light.

Let there be one to share the lone moments
And flames to brighten a lonely grate,
Let salty tears from the wild wind's eyes
Be gathered in monsoon's mad outburst.

Let there be drumbeats in silent shrines
To awaken the fiery goddess in me,
Let the mysteries of turmoil be flung to the lyre
And death bequeath me another life.

Let there be ravaging solitude in me
And lush, ravishing dreams anew,
Let there be one to witness all change
And alone, alone shall I wither away.

Maya Davi Chalissery

One Day

And then one day
We'll see each other.
You'll be busy, so will I
And yet, we'll hold each other's eye.

No words will be spoken
No pleasantries exchanged
No stories of days gone by shared
And yet, we'll know everything.

What we waited for
The hope that we secretly held
The dream we could not let go
Would then pass by us happily.

And then we'll part
One body, one soul
No distances, no bounds, no rules
Would keep us away.

Mridula Robert

Demonetized

Standing, waiting in an endless line
To be doled out a pittance from his own savings,
He looked up at the ruthless sun
Glaring down as if wreaking vengeance
On the poor souls who shared his tiresome wait.
His dreams were wilting faster than his crops,
As the power which made the country go round
Twirled the fate of powerless millions.
His thoughts reeled and his head spun,
Hours of thirst, hunger and restlessness
Gracelessly escorted him
To a cashless, hunger-less world.

Nandita Nair

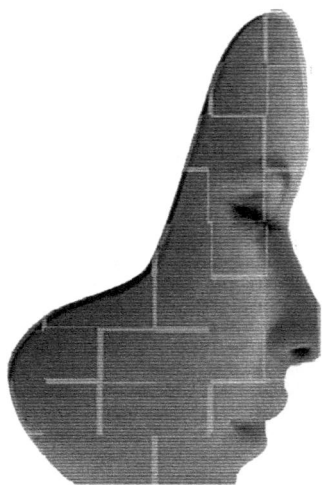

Thirst

I was without a face
and you touched me.

You know how this goes:

You are the wine in the grape,
the raw breath of fresh roses,
a whole almond

I touch the branches of the night,
graze against the wrinkled body of the tree,
gaze at the crystal moon,
Everything brings me to you.

The falling leaves of this slow autumn,
the stale morning bread,
The dusty rack of souvenirs:
You fill everything.

Sometimes I love you
and even my soul is wet.

Jackfruit

The way I learned
to eat chakkapazham[1]
in Trivandrum :
I use my teeth
to tear into the yellow
flowers, suck out the gold
in the fibrous heart
with my tongue.
I let the juice spill,
dribble down my chin.

January mornings,
the hard fruit
is brought to our door.
Afternoons, when the elders are asleep,
we enjoy it
outside in the lazy sun.
For hours we bite
we suck
until the ka, sap,
is sticky all over our hands.

So tonight,
When he tells me to suck
and find the core
with my tongue,
I pretend
that this is my first taste
of that formidable fruit.
I imagine us outside,
carving our way through
the thorny jackfruit.

---

1   Malayalam for jackfruit,

Neena P

Peregrination

Being a fantasy child,
My Childhood was spent in the Wonderlands, Treasure Islands and
Baskervilles.
I was cast in Multifarious characters
The fantastic Alice of nonsense,
The Jim who sailed me away to treasure hunt,
The Holmesian deduction which drew me to reality.
Thrown I was into the netherworld of science,
Mixing this, twirling this,
Adding this till I get a 'Drink me'!
Chemistry vanquished my Alice into thin air.
The cockroach prince in the plate implored:
Need a kiss to break this curse!
Chants of Dissection pulsated every nook and cranny,
Escape velocity propelled my Holmes into an unknown orbit,
Fantastic me become faceless me.
Tiresome, tedious three years of dejection
Determined to regain my identity,
Drilled out all the eccentricities,
Re Kindled fantasies, revived imaginations.
Lost in the magical wood of literature,
I'm waiting to be reborn.

Nisha Francis Alapatt

A Girl

"A Girl…"
Father frowned
Mother sobbed
Good luck!
A boy next time!!

My birth circumscribed my life
From dawn to dusk
Denying me
The sun, the moon
And the shining stars.

Girls don't laugh
Girls don't talk loud
Girls are weak
The do's and don'ts
And compulsions in abundance.

Is the daylight dim
And nights even darker
Only because I was born a girl?

Radhika Menon

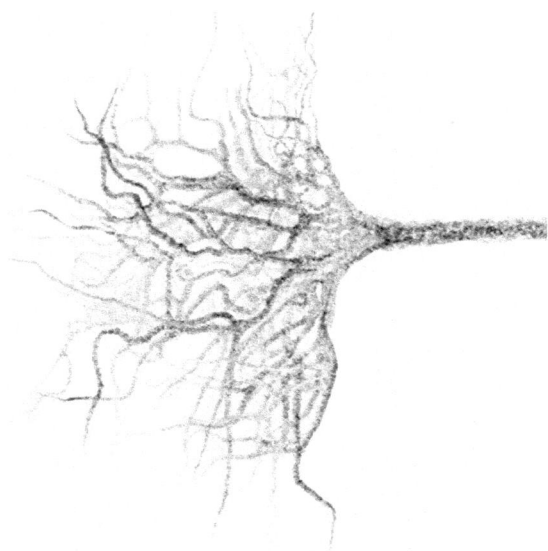

Uprooted

You might be unaware
For you walk in the shade
Sheltered, under our pain.

We are the past
Our land was sacred.
Our scriptures were ancient
Our identity was divine.

Histories bore you fast,
Legends sore you hard
Epics leave you sad.
Thousand times you sin,
Disorder trips you in.

The silent graveyard awaits
For, new inhabitants to settle.
Nature woven in vain
Curses the day in disdain.
Our land turns barren
While our lives melt in oblivion.

When, darkness seduces you
Shadows immerse you.
When the soul pleads you to pray,
Innocence shuns you away.
We leave you to your fate,
For you cremated us
Even before, we could awake.

Sea And Shore Never Meet

He never knew I possessed a soul.
When he touched,
It didn't make any difference
Clinging to each other we lay tangled.

Between extremities
When my breath became heavy
He broke off
Believing his passion was replete.

Alas, he knows not
Remorseful soul remains numb
A toy trapped in a child's hand
The body is just a host.

Ah… that abundance of breath
The tumult of our passion
And the pure bliss of mating
Echo endlessly in my now deaf ears.

Our memories consume me.
As the sun sinks into the sea,
And painstakingly I realize
The sea and shore never meet!

The Basement Of Memories

Yesterday I was only six
When the clock cried sex.

Today pimples sprouted on my face
As I started to ache.

Sharp nails stood as soldiers do
When wandering eyes rested on my breast.

Scarlet stained teeth gleamed
As I walked alone.

Cold street lights shrieked
When vulturine humans shredded me into bits.

Distressed Night, draped me in its gown,
As I lay curled inside a trench.

None moaned over my distressed state.
Alas, the sad account hid restfully,

In the basement of memories
Where all the losses are stored away.

Shani Fasil

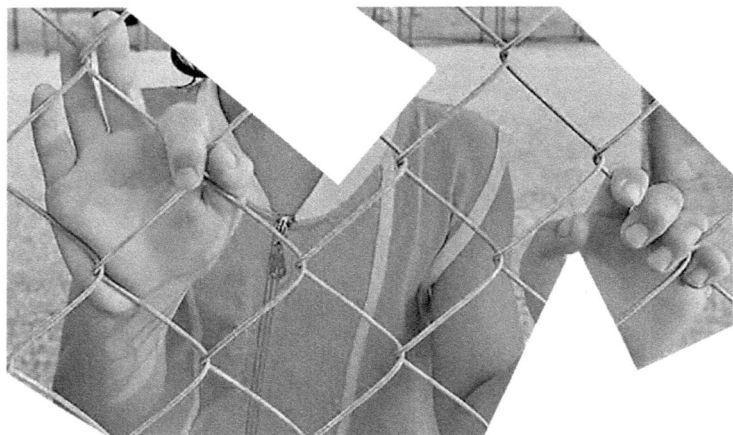

Refugee

Well defined inside your boundaries
You can choose to ignore us.
You can name the land
Amidst the barbed wires
And call it yours.
Fruits of death
Ripen and explode.
And we, hollow souls
Exist like shadows.
The same Exodus,
But without Moses.
You need not tell us
There's no Promised Land.

Trespassers to be prosecuted.
We become insane with endless
Waiting outside your fence.
With starving babies
Sucking at our empty breasts.
We bear one name
In Syria, Afghanistan, everywhere.
We don't dream
Of home anymore.
Lost among the
Latitudes and longitudes you draw
We only speak the
Language of sorrow.

I Am Beyond You

I will be back one day,
After a long hibernation
Inside strange burrows
Of silence,
After everything
Has taken its toll
And has gone
After the flood recedes
Coward? Me?
How can one escape from existing?
Nothing will change
Even after a thousand years.
We shall hate
And love and wait…
I am no Ulysses,
But a woman with dreams.
My mind can travel across
Space, time and boundaries.
Don't bind me,
In one shape
One costume, one color…
What you see as my truth
Let me be.
Don't try to identify me,
To collect my residue
From your vague memories,
I am just a stranger.
Farther than your imagination
I am beyond you.

Sheeba Thattil

To Return Unto Dust

Hear my plea
Set me free
My stifled sobs
Speak for me;
Imprisoned in a jar
I float like a bean
A lifeless stone
In a stagnant pool,
Flushed from the womb
That gifted me life
Designed to be
A specimen encased;
Imprisoned in a jar
I float like a bean
Reminder of guilt
To a murderous race,
Distorted and disfigured
I strike against glass
''Release me'' I groan
To return unto dust.

Sands On Fire

Incited to horror
On desolate sands
Soiled forms survive
The slaughter of death;
Oppressed with fear
And packed with corpses
The burning sands watch
The pattern shift;
Formless images
Strike the void
In quest of salvation
From Eastern sands;

Portents of discord
Torment the stillness
Wedged between 'Powers'
Hostile shapes conspire.

Burnt At The Stake

A flaming giant rose
Bloomed in the morning sky
Shedding tangled thorns;
Plucked from my breast
And pierced through the heart
The twins were burnt at the stake;
Scorched by its flames
The rose bush collapsed
Into the abyss wide;
My first-born was dismembered
And deformed for life
The stake didn't burn her through.

Ravaged Orchards

The elusive morn
In tremulous strides,
Through gazing orchards
Of luminous green;
In breathless stillness
The oceans wake,
And sedate streams
Rise up in waves;
With furtive glances
And seductive sighs,
Her colossal length
In tremors quake;
Deep, ghastly rumblings
And smoldering rage,
The morning calm shatters
In a chorus of screams;
The delusive eve
In faltering strides,
Through ravaged orchards
Of dubious grey.

Partners In Crime

Bread and bombs
Scale down with force
Competing in vain
Through Eastern skies;
Strange companions
Partners in crime
On diverse missions
Together in flight.
The baskets are filled
With bread and bombs
The will to live
Yet lingers on;
Swept by the current
The baskets float
Through oceans of hate
To distant shores.

The Seventh Star

Thrown by fate
On thorny paths
The trio walked
With measured strides;
Scarred and lonely,
Sunk in colourless sand,
Seventeen milestones
Lined the path.

Through the indistinct haze
Of the darkened skies
A silent flicker
Gleamed with life;
Shadows danced
Across the skies
The Seventh Star
Spread a gentle light.

In God's Own Country

My heart aches for a draught of sweet drink
Fresh from the swaying green coconut palms,
Refreshingly intoxicating, the breathtaking flavor
Never ceases to fascinate the fervent traveler,
A drink designed to enchant the animated mind
Its pleasurable sweetness caresses the taste buds.

As dusk descends on the serene back-waters of Kerala
The anchored house-boat, rests idly on the calm waters,
On the bow, an earthen pot dances , in explicable ecstasy
With the lapping of the water against the sides of the boat.
Each sip of God's plenty from God's Own Country
Brings an incredible sense, of peace, to my weary mind.

Sheeji Raphael

Void

A giant cavern, ogres,
Gaping heads, lolling tongues,
Breaking into splinters,
Glittering in the teardrops,
Drenched in sweat and mucus,
Spitting fury, froth and venom
Pulling apart, tearing ---

Lost in the entwined shapes,
Legs and arms, mouths,
A chewed out piece, shameless,
The anguish, the laments, moans,
Dancing in the death throes,
There, searching for myself
The rescue, a mirage----

Sunil Ravindran

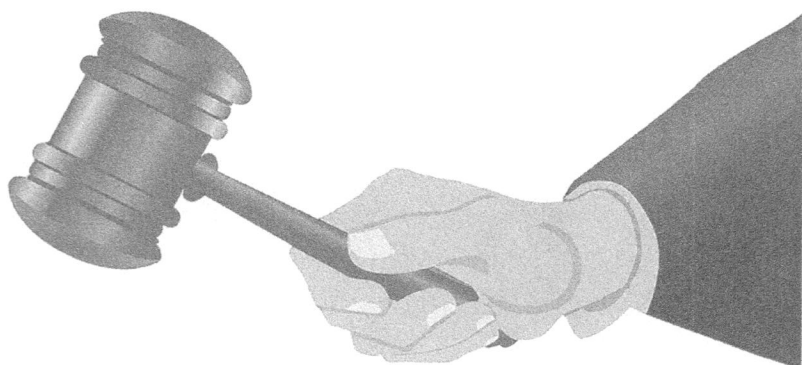

Judges Uncalled

Get ready to don the black satin robe,
bring down the gavel with scorn and disdain.

This is no more than a reel of frames to you.
A painting to interpret, a poem waiting to be discerned.

Forget you were never there in person, all those times
when you spoke too soon, this moment if you just felt

the nausea of silence. Cared for frozen tears on their faces.
When the earth crumbled and men were swatted like flies

unscathed as you were, still were you the ordained one?
Walk through the labyrinth we all passed once, to get here.

Limbs lying strewn, blood dried on the tattered railings.
Splattered flesh of once sprightly men and women. Smell death.

A wrong turn is all it took, You were there once my friend,
and you never even knew it.

Yet, the show tonight is cast wrong and you get to play God.
Kneel before that altar. Waiting to be vilified.
when they knew, their best will never be good enough for you.

A Twisted Landing

My long frame cramped and blended in with the coach seat.
There is a tranquility I seek, even up at thirty thousand feet.
Not that I had no premonitions that moment,
A sepulchral hum from the engines amidst the roar;
I sure saw wraiths of vapor and smoke outside, curling
in strange shapes, as we lifted off to the evening skies.

It started off like poisoned rats scampering in the attic,
the shrieks did come from the tail, I was certain.
Odd thing it was, there was no trace of a panic,
the drink carts rolled, a man even asked for gin with tonic.

The twilight sky applied hue to a brackish black in a jiffy.
Bolts of blitz cut the wafer air like butter.
It rained pellets, which were the size of golf balls.
Then we were rocked. Side to Side, Up and down.
Once. Twice. And another eighteen times.
Chants and yells floated through the cabin,
of course, we had faith and despair in equal measure.
Even babies in bassinets joined the chorus mayhem,
Why wouldn't they? It was a big fun ride for them.

My lungs on fire, I looked for any land below,
only plumes of black smoke in its stead.
This puppy has "Fly-by-wire", I am reminded,
even a macaque can command this and manoeuvre.

Eons replete with thumps and clunks had elapsed
before the tires kissed asphalt threaded by white bands.
Someone screamed "c'mon now", and the damn brakes were hit.
The tube convulsed and screeched to a halt.
Even the believers were too wasted to clap.

A Father's Ode

Thousands of daffodils glowing golden this day,
my precious bundle of joy turns eight today.

The first time I ever saw him, I still remember,
wrapped in white, the boy was in a deep slumber.

His lips were red, his black hair had a shine,
he had a nose that looked exactly like mine.

With long trembling hands, I had held him tight,
the heavens must have smiled at his father's delight.

One cold winter withered and went by,
then came the beautiful spring God sent by.

The blooms and the birds watched with glee,
when he took his first step and looked at me.

Time, as they say rarely does stall,
my little boy has grown and become real tall.

With a joyous heart and a tear in my eye,
Wish you the best ahead, oh my dear boy!

Sometimes!

Sometimes I shudder and gasp for breath,
tortured and wounded with thousands of cuts

Those stares from the corner of her eyes,
they are daggers
poisoned with a snake woman's charm.

They sting and burn, whether I am far away
or caressing her soft slender arm.

Sometimes though awake, I am in a trance,
throat parched and dry when she is in her seductive prance

those quivering lips and swaying hips,
and words are shrapnel
laden with shards of deception that harm,

time will march on, though the pain will still linger,
hurt, locked up will always remain warm.

Sushane Parthan

Silver Jack

Perched atop a familial seat,
Perilously close to a familiar sight,
The lone seaman breathed-in the dew,
Bathed by the off-white half-light.

In the metal wreck ahead, gleamed,
The pearly sinews of Her fallen first-mate.
Reflected in the lunar lumen,
A resplendent gentleman of ill-fate.

I yelled to him, "Respected Sir,
Why dost thou not leave Her behind?
Surely wouldst be a bloody burden, to not,
Pass on and be around One's own kind."

The wise old Officer replied,
"Lad, thou hast much to learn.
Technology might have far bettered me,
But by the Seven Seas didst I earn.

"Look up and out, across the western sky,
Orion sits; awaiting his early demise.
Cradled by the melancholic moon,
Eluding infinite eyes; worldwide skies.

"Seamen worldwide watch with bated breath.
Their solitary comrade sinking into the sea,
Their soulmate biting the dust.
Now as lone as alone can be.

"You, too, lad; mourn his fall,
Mourn his end before us all.
For thou will find bitter loneliness,
'Til the setting of the blazing ball."

And as the pearly sinews precipitated to the rocks,
The lone seaman opened his red eyes.
Solitary, sober, solely surviving,
Searching for a comrade in the skies.

Context

The added advantage of pursuing Science,
Is the application of Mathematics, Physics and Chemistry.
Some of the biggest lessons in life are learned,
from Acceleration Due To Gravity.

Nature giveth to Man variable mass,
And relative sizes to create misproportions.
And thus came the equation of Gravitational Force,
Requisite to calculate orbital distortions.

But how dost this matter to Me, You may ask?
This is Science, not an Elixir for Life's ills.
Ah, Perspective is the answer to your question, My Friend!
The realisation might give your groin the chills.

So this, thus, began a day of exploration. Consider this:
If $2A + 2B = 2C$,
Then surely $A + B = C$, as well.
Because all we do is divide by 2. You see?

Now that's a given, I know. All that the rhyme does,
Is gracefully weighten something so light.
But all that I did is lay the foundation,
A premise; I do believe that is my right.

But on a given day, something's amiss:
$2A + B =$ Question Mark.
Now, wait a minute! There's something amiss,
Seems like some misappropriation in the dark.

It seems that into the space of 2A, strode,
A single, befuddled B; all alone.
Or could it be that the 2A crashed in,
Bossing around in the lone B's zone?

Whatever be the cause of this disaster,
The question now is: What is the fix?
If it were imperative to restore normalcy,
Do we add or subtract, betwixt?

Let two individuals share two qualities,
Two features, two habits or two assets.
And let, in their kinship, said two objects be imperative,
Forming necessitated, soldering sets.

If one of the said objects didst disappear,
By factors untold, uncontrolled.
Then what shalt be the best action or recourse,
To avoid meandering in the nightly cold?

Said the 2A: "Oh, 2B! Where didst thou disappear?
I long for your warmth, My Friend!
Thou art such a warm and beautiful person, 2B...
No. This can't be... This shalt not be the end!"

"For I will repress, sacrificing myself,
Shedding half of my skin, for thee."
Hence $2A / 2 = A$; that is suicide.
Nevertheless not in vain, for $A + B = C$.

But tiny little B didst speak out in mock anger,
"How could you even think of that, you fool?!
All that remains is half your strength, your widsom,
Half the beast; now you're only half as cool."

"Under your tutelage and care, have I grown to be,
The person I am today, for them all to see.
How, then, can you abandon, in a manner so cowardly,
50 percent of the self that means so much to me?"

"For, under your knowledge and the smile affixed beneath,
Have I grown, from ashes to gashes, fold by fold.
And thus I will arise once again, My Friend,
And what's more, I will grow twofold!"

And thus, under the dark brown covers at night,
Didst a miracle of untold dimensions occur.
Look! $2A + 2B = 2C$ again,
Providing academicians the world over some succour.

And thus, my statement I do reiterate,
If you wanted to consider it, you could.
Some of the biggest lessons in life are learned,
From Simple Mathematics. Point proved.

High And Low

Six hours separate them.
One of the ascendency and the other of demise.
Borne to transient lunarcy,
Of invisible, immiscible skies.

Six hours separate them.
One of sensual swells harbouring thunderous knells.
The other of voluminous drops hoarding roaring kops,
Both chiming their crashing bells.

Twelve hours separate them.
Tooth for tooth, an eye for an eye.
The swirling axes of the distant pearly orb ensure,
That, twelve hours later, another will come by.

And thus, in twenty four hours we see four,
All repetitions of highs and lows.
All knocking at our seaward doors.
As this morning, low tide comes and goes.

Vijay Nair

Passion Fruit Lips

Beyond this moment, our universe
Will be bursting at its seams - -
A gypsy light dances under this train
And among the trees along the coast.

Love, is love a stunning sea-nymph
Rising with the majestic waves
Disappearing with the angry foam?
I ask as I sit down by your side

You throw me an uncertain look
As you stroke your midnight hair
Swimming to your shapely hips
And I can sense a gathering storm

In your eyes, crossing the bridge
Of your nose - - and it subsides
When I inhale your scent and crush
Your passionate, passion fruit lips.

A Man Who Knows His God

To lose a part of a lung
At twenty-two and still stick
To the path you rightly chose - -

To look at suffering in the eye
And say: "This city does not know
How to cry", and not step back - -

To speak about things the past
Pretended not to see - -
To cross the border of the will

And bring back some of those
Who had lost all hope,
Is a gesture that resonates

Uncommon in troubled times:
So different from those who came before,
You are a man who knows his God.

Lost Paradise

This year too angels in white and white
Shall flap their wings and land with folded palms
Walking through the gates of our minds
With celestial smiles, reminding us
Of another vision of Paradise

We shall be blessed to witness: all we get to glimpse
With uncommon sense are wandering files
Seduced by dust and a shroud of mist,
Of wrinkled promises and the farmer
Strung up in the harvest of his debts.

All we get to see are crimson rivers
Drying up in the widow's eyes
And the cry and the old raspy voice
Of God's giver of life on Earth
When they brought him covered

And the crowd let him pass through
The gates of a Lost Paradise.

A Book

You can't place a flimsy bookmark
Between the pages of her life:
You must read her.

Between hardbound covers
Without the semblance of a pause
Without dog-earing her thoughts.

She knows her style will survive
A million readers and more
Being always but herself and no one else.

She is the prologue and the epilogue
Of every poignant story ever told
And God has written her blurb.

Wedded Silence

One thing about death
Is certain: it is a time
To share

At someone else's funeral
The unwavering stare of grief
At another's annual absence

And the tired curse
Of sudden fickle distances
Travelled by the heart's

''Dearly beloved''
Who have assembled there
In the witnessing drizzle

To be one with
The living and the dead
And an earth-splattered

Wedded silence.

Publisher's Note

The great response for Poemlets 15 has inspired us to continue with the mission of bringing some more great poetry to light.

In this edition, we bring poetry from these great poets: Aswathy Balachandran, Beena Job, Geethanjali Kurian, Joe Poonolly, O.J Joycee, Lakshmi Russell, Latha Nair R, Lisa John, Lovji KN, Mabel Susan, Mallika A Nair, Maya Davi Chalissery, Mridula Robert, Nandita Nair, Neena P, Nisha Francis Alapatt, Radhika Menon, Shani Fasil, Sheeba Thattil, Sheeji Raphael, Sunil Ravindran, Sushane Parthan and Vijay Nair. Thank you for sharing your fantasy, your dreams, your anxiety, your thoughts… and for extracting the essence of those feelings to a few lines so that we could drop it into this book and present it to the world.

We are thankful to "Poemlets", the Facebook global community, where it all started and which keeps us going.

Isabel has done it again. The image on the cover of this book is her charcoal sketch. Thanks Isabel. (She had also designed the cover of Poemlets 15).

The entire credit for making this book possible goes to its editor Sheeba Thattil. Her resources and connections are beyond 'amazing'. Please accept our appreciation for all your hard work.

Here is Poemlets 16 and more to come!

Sound Vision Media
www.soundvision.media
Ewing, NJ, USA